THE SUPER SCIENCE BOOK OF OUR BODIES

Graham Peacock and Terry Hudson

Freckles

*Very last thing late at night, I wished my freckles out of sight,
Prayed that they would fade away, never see the light of day.
When falling heavy into sleep, my nightmares crept on stealthy feet,
A mirror beckoned through the gloom, across a desert once my room.
But when I reached it, nothing there. No face, nor arms, nor legs, no hair.
No ears, no eyes, I couldn't see the funny face that once was me.*

*And as I wept a dragon came, through forests green with tongue aflame
He said my tears were magic rain, to bring my freckles back again
He cast a spell. Dark rain clouds grew. It poured and poured. Celestial dew
Falling on the mirror speckles, raining back familiar freckles.*

by Catherine Baxter

Illustrations by Frances Lloyd

Thomson Learning
New York

Books in the Super Science series

The Environment
Light
Materials
Our Bodies
Time
Weather

First published in the
United States in 1993 by
Thomson Learning
115 Fifth Avenue
New York, NY 10003

First published in 1993 by
Wayland (Publishers) Ltd

Library of Congress Cataloging-in-Publication Data applied for

ISBN: 1-56847-023-1
Printed in Italy

Series Editor: Cally Chambers
Designer: Loraine Hayes Design

Picture acknowledgments

Illustrations by Frances Lloyd.
Cover illustration by Martin Gordon.

Photographs by permission of: Allsport 28; Rex Features 21, 29; Science Photo Library 4 (Biology Media), 5 (Mehau Kulyk), 6 (David Scharf), 8 (bottom, Astrid & Hanns Frieder Michler), 9 (James Stevenson), 11 (Lawrence Migdale), 14 (James Stevenson), 15 (top, Adam Hart Davis/bottom, Martin Dohrn), 16 (Manfred Kage), 18 (Manfred Kage), 20 (Simon Fraser), 22 (top, Will and Demi MclIntyre/bottom, Blair Seitz), 26 (top, CNRI/bottom, National Library of Medicine), 27 (John Durham); Tony Stone Worldwide 7 (top, Dave Saunders/bottom), 8 (top), 12, 13, 17 (top, Ed Pritchard/bottom, Adrian Masters), 25 (Peter Correz); Topham 7 (bottom right); Wayland Picture Library 10, 13 (top), 15 (top), 19, 23: Zefa 15 (top).

CONTENTS

BODY CELLS

Our bodies are the most important things in our lives. People come in all shapes and sizes, but we are all made up of the same bits and pieces, and we all "work" in the same way.

For a start, all living things are made up of cells. Cells are very small, but when they are joined together they form plants and animals. We can think of cells as the building blocks of our bodies.

All animal cells need ▶ food and oxygen. The food is needed to give cells energy to repair themselves and grow. Oxygen is needed to break down the food. Animals that are made up of only one cell—like this amoeba—do not have any problems getting food and oxygen into the cell, or taking waste out of it. The chemicals simply pass through its outer layer, called the cell membrane.

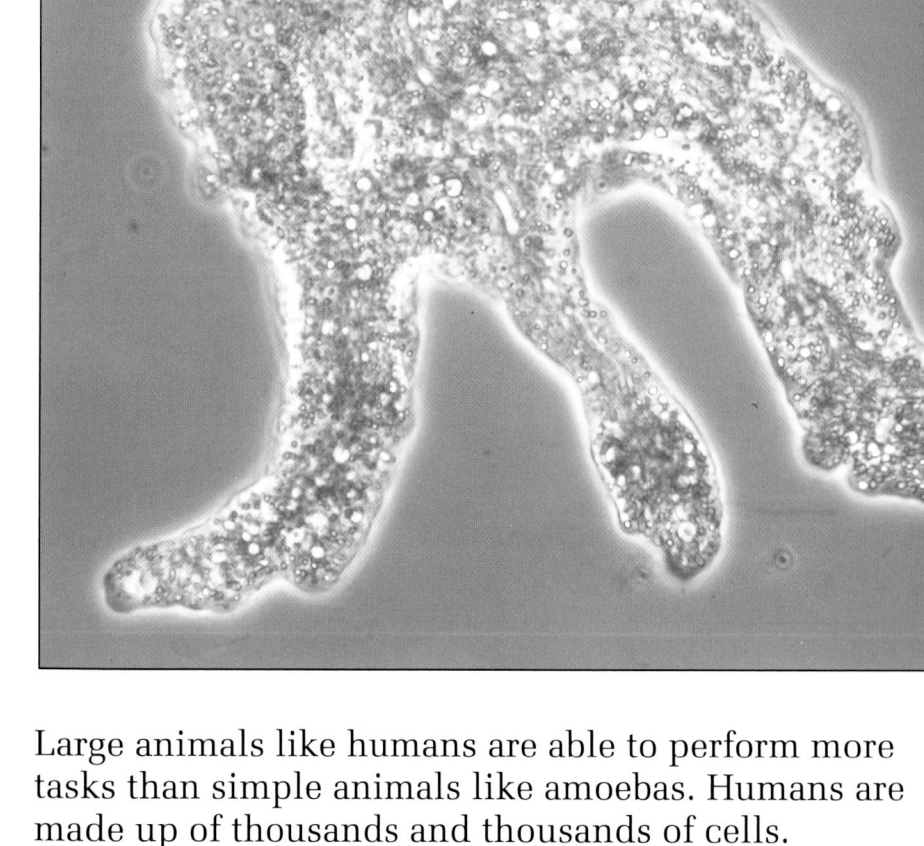

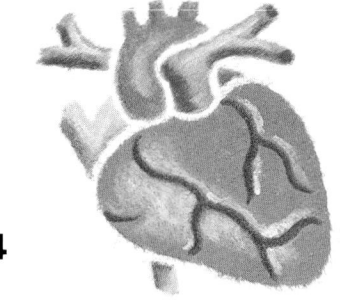

Large animals like humans are able to perform more tasks than simple animals like amoebas. Humans are made up of thousands and thousands of cells. Different cells do different jobs. For example, there are skin cells, hair cells, and muscle cells. Because a lot of the cells are deep inside our bodies, we have special systems to transport food and oxygen to them, and to take waste away from them. If this did not happen, the cells would die.

◀ Cells that are grouped together to do the same job are called tissues. Tissues that are grouped together can do more than one job. Groups of tissues make up the organs in your body such as your heart and your liver.

4

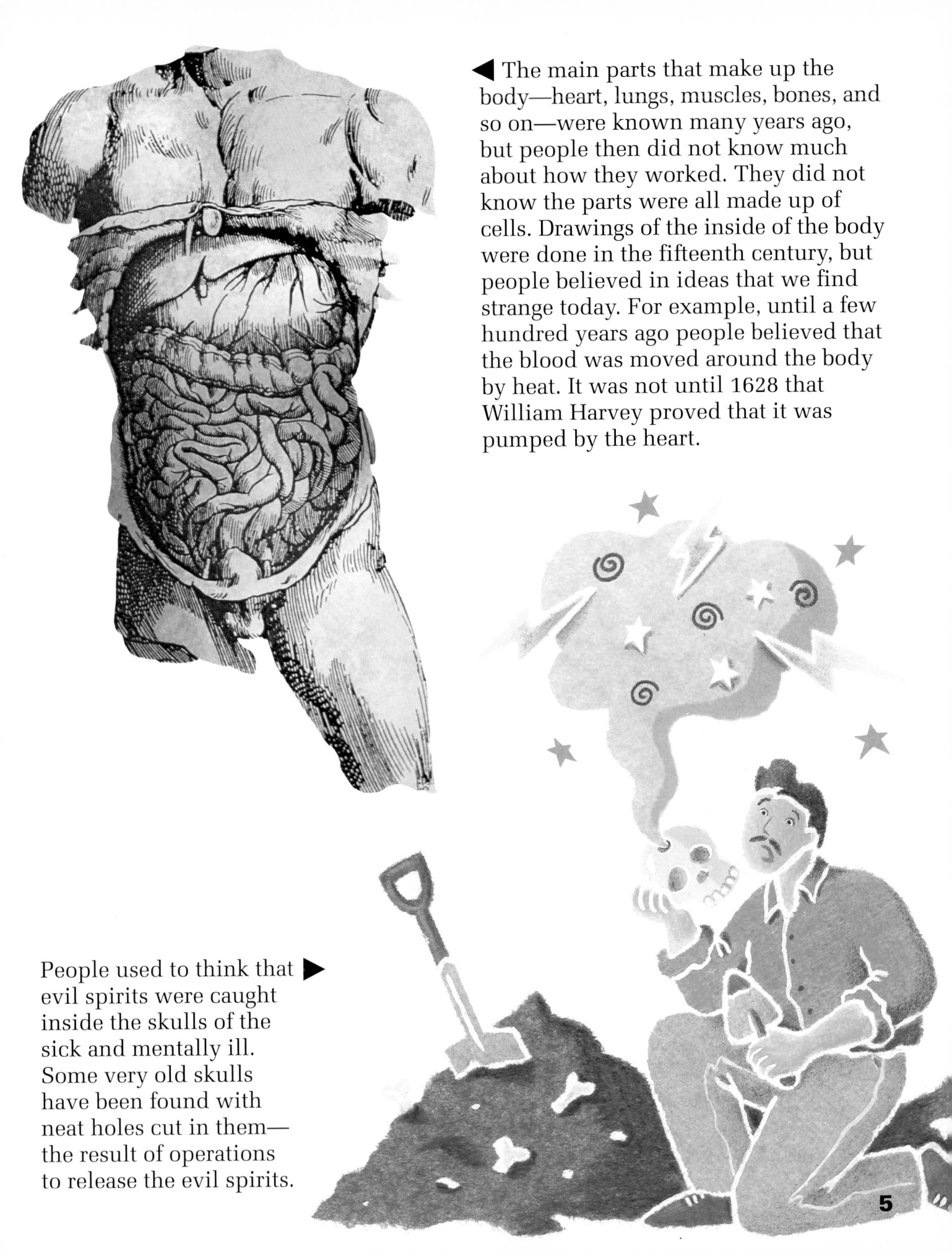

◀ The main parts that make up the body—heart, lungs, muscles, bones, and so on—were known many years ago, but people then did not know much about how they worked. They did not know the parts were all made up of cells. Drawings of the inside of the body were done in the fifteenth century, but people believed in ideas that we find strange today. For example, until a few hundred years ago people believed that the blood was moved around the body by heat. It was not until 1628 that William Harvey proved that it was pumped by the heart.

People used to think that ▶ evil spirits were caught inside the skulls of the sick and mentally ill. Some very old skulls have been found with neat holes cut in them— the result of operations to release the evil spirits.

THE SKIN

◀ Your skin is like a large waterproof bag. It helps to hold all of the parts of your body in place. It also helps to keep you warm when it is cold and cool when it is hot. Your skin has an outer covering of dead cells. If you look at this microscope photograph of human skin, you can see that the top layer of dead cells are like tiny roof tiles. This is to help keep harmful substances away from the rest of the skin.

The skin of an average size adult weighs about 4.5 lbs. If it was stretched out, it would cover an area of about 20 sq. ft. – that is about as big as a double bed! You can figure out the area of the skin on the palms of your hands or the soles of your feet by drawing around them on graph paper. By counting the squares, you can get an idea of the area. ▶

Skin glands produce a salty liquid called sweat. The sweat wets your skin in hot weather. As it evaporates, it cools the surface of your skin. You can test this for yourself by licking your finger and then blowing on it.

Your skin can also protect itself from strong sunlight by making a dark substance called melanin. This is why some people are born with black or brown skins, and why other pale-skinned people become tan in sunny weather.

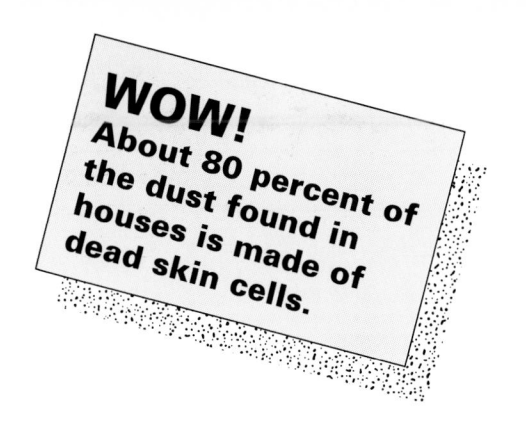

WOW!
About 80 percent of the dust found in houses is made of dead skin cells.

Your skin is covered in a thin layer of grease. This makes it waterproof and helps to protect it from germs. Dirt gets trapped in the greasy layer and can be hard to wash away. Today we use soap to remove the grease and dirt. Before soap was invented, people had other methods of removing dirt from their skins. The Romans used a piece of slate and water to scrape themselves clean. A few hundred years ago, people believed that bathing could weaken you, and so bathing was not as common as it is now. Perfumes were made to cover up the smell of people who had not bathed for a long time.

The hair that grows from your ▲ ▶ skin helps to keep you warm. The way you style the hair on your head can say a lot about how you feel about yourself. Many people also decorate their skin because of religion or fashion.

THE SKELETON

The frame of bones inside your body is called your skeleton. Your skeleton supports you and gives you your shape. Without it, you would not be able to stand up or move. Your bones are column-shaped, which makes them very strong.

The large pillars in this ▶ ancient Greek temple are column-shaped and can support many tons of rock. They are solid and very heavy. Bones are not solid. They are full of little hollow spaces, so they are very light.

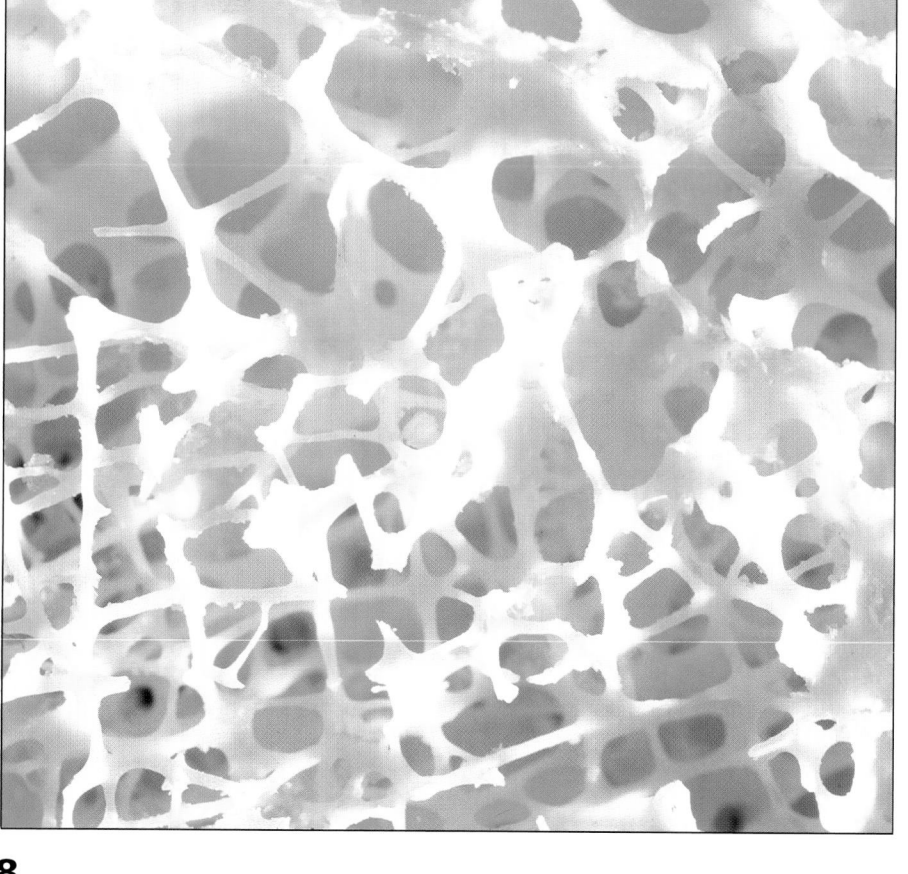

◀ Bone is also the place where blood cells are made. These are made in the honeycomb spaces in the middle of the bone (pictured here). The jellylike material that makes the blood cells is called bone marrow. There are also cells in the bones that make repairs. These cells build a layer around the damaged part of the bone and protect it as it is being slowly mended. After the damaged bone has healed, the protective layer is gradually broken down.

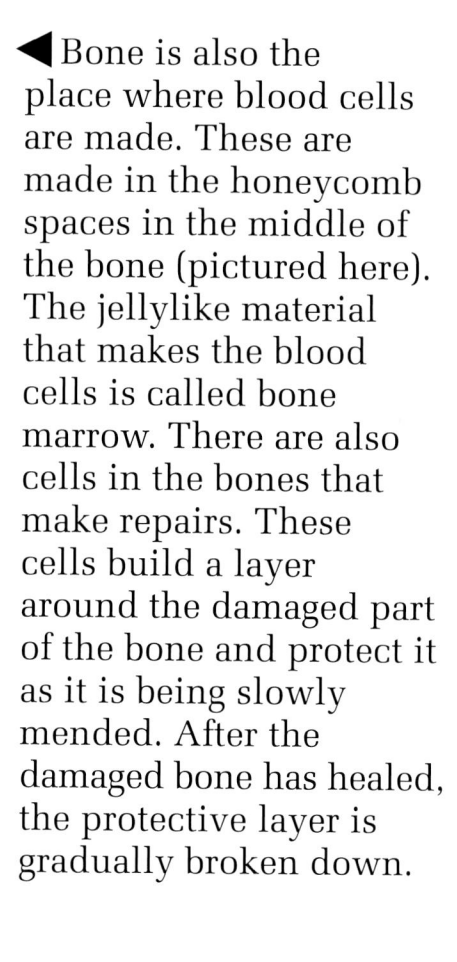

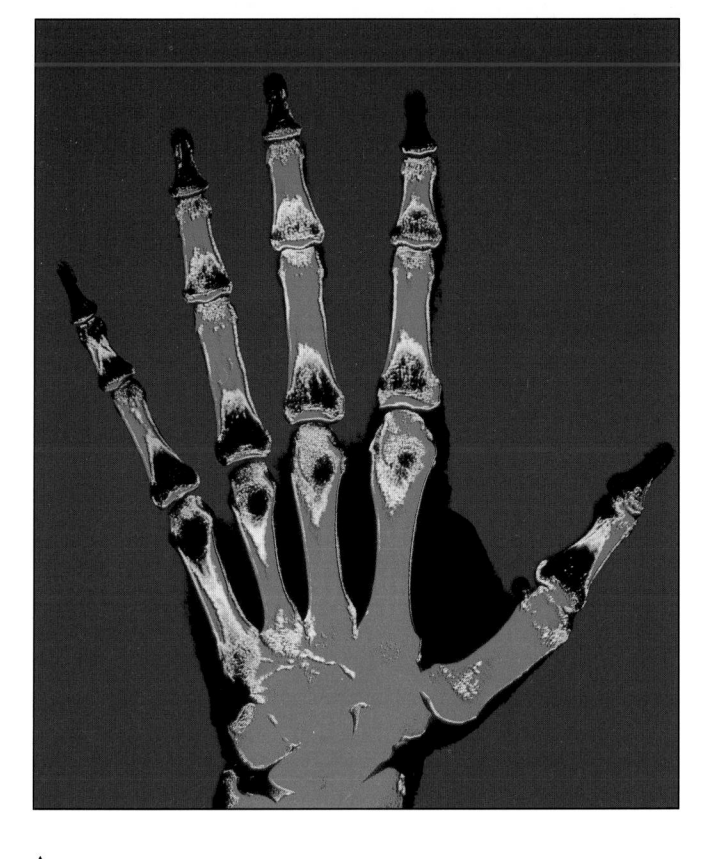

▲ Skeletons are often used in horror movies and books to frighten people. The pirate flag is a skull and crossbones, and the destination of Jim Hawkins and Long John Silver in *Treasure Island* is Skeleton Island.

▲ To let your body move, each bone links with others at joints. This X ray shows the joints in your fingers. To protect the ends of the bones where they meet at the joint, they are covered by a softer tissue called cartilage and are surrounded by an oily fluid. This fluid works in the same way as oil on a bicycle chain.

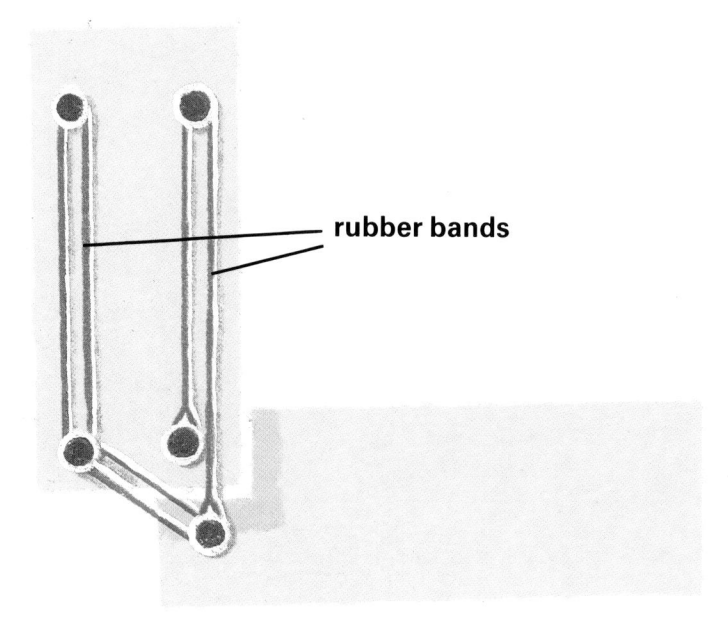

rubber bands

Bones are moved by muscles that are attached to the bone by tendons. As the muscle contracts (tightens) the bone is pulled. To move the bone back, a different set of muscles pull in the opposite direction. Muscles cannot push; they can only pull. Some people spend a lot of time exercising to increase the size of their muscles.

Make a Model Arm ▲

1 Cut out two long, rectangular shapes from cardboard. Position five paper fasteners as shown.
2 Connect the shapes together with two rubber bands.
3 Bend the model arm and see how the rubber bands work like muscles.

DIGESTION

Your body is like a machine. It needs energy to run, and it regularly needs to have parts repaired or replaced. To do this, your body uses food. The food cannot be used as it appears on the plate. The pieces are much too big to pass into your body. The food must be broken down. This breaking down of food is called digestion, and it takes place in a number of steps.

WOW! If you pulled out your intestines into a long line, they would stretch farther than the world long jump record.

◀ When you chew food, it is broken into smaller pieces by your teeth. The sharp front teeth help to bite and cut the food into smaller pieces. The flatter, back teeth grind the food down into a paste that can be swallowed. Chewing also lets a liquid called saliva mix with the food. This liquid wets the food so that it can be swallowed, and it also starts to break it down by chemical reaction. Chemicals that break down food are called enzymes. Each enzyme breaks down a certain type of food.

In the stomach, the food is mixed with acid and more enzymes so that it is broken down into smaller and smaller pieces. After mixing for about four hours, the food passes into a part of the small intestine called the duodenum, which is about 10 inches long. Here even more enzymes are added to break down the food. The food is now very soft and wet, and it is small enough to be taken into your bloodstream.

▼

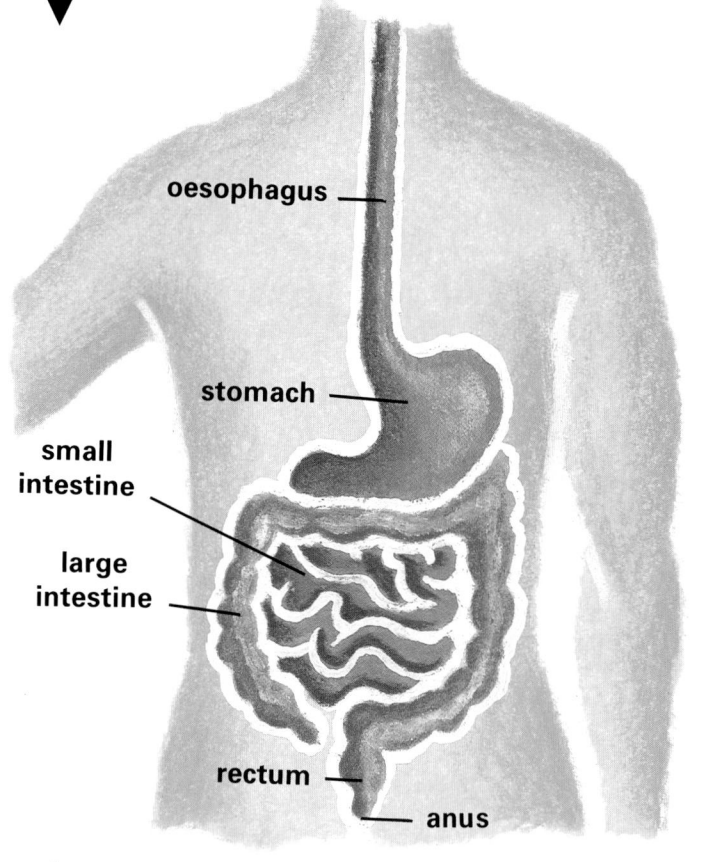

oesophagus

stomach

small intestine

large intestine

rectum

anus

▲ After the duodenum, the food goes farther along the small intestine. The small intestine is narrow, but it is nearly 20 feet long. It has many folds that catch the food as it passes. Once it has been trapped, the food passes through the wall of the intestine and into the bloodstream. Any remaining food is passed out of the body as waste. The journey from the mouth to the end of the intestine is about 30 feet.

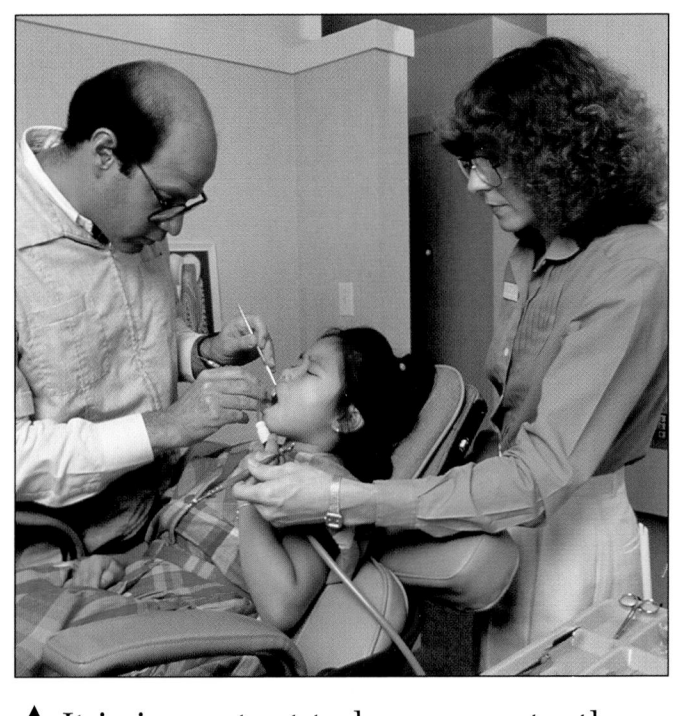

▲ It is important to keep your teeth healthy by brushing them regularly and by visiting the dentist. If you leave food on your teeth for too long, it can help bacteria to grow. This bacteria can produce acids that attack your teeth and gums. This causes pain and may mean that your teeth have to be filled or even taken out. Other parts of the digestive system can also cause problems. Sometimes, too much acid in the stomach causes acid indigestion. Sodium bicarbonate (an alkali) can be taken to balance the extra acid.

HEALTHY EATING

It is important that you eat enough different kinds of food to give your body the correct amount of energy and chemicals. If you are lucky enough to live where there is plenty of food, then this is usually no problem. However, not all people can get enough food. This makes them very ill, and many die.

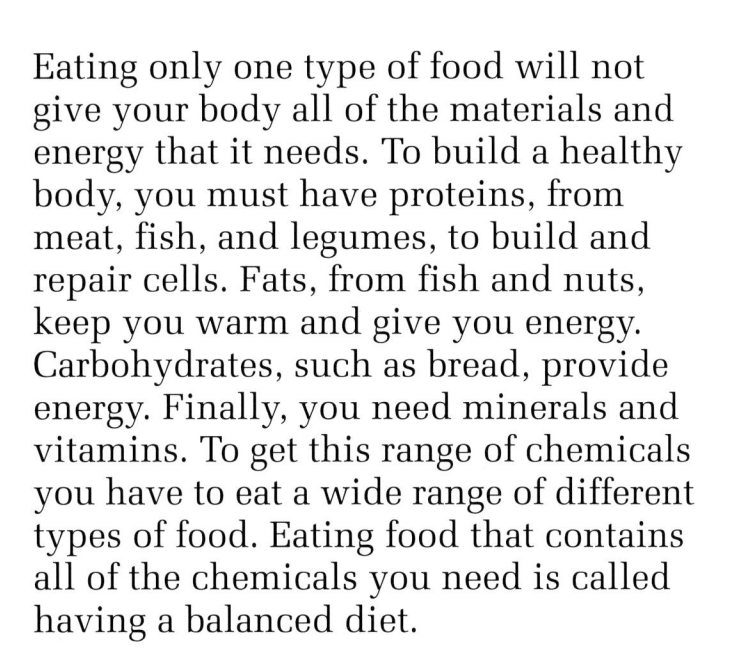

WOW!
The food that an average person eats during a lifetime weighs as much as twenty rhinos.

Eating only one type of food will not give your body all of the materials and energy that it needs. To build a healthy body, you must have proteins, from meat, fish, and legumes, to build and repair cells. Fats, from fish and nuts, keep you warm and give you energy. Carbohydrates, such as bread, provide energy. Finally, you need minerals and vitamins. To get this range of chemicals you have to eat a wide range of different types of food. Eating food that contains all of the chemicals you need is called having a balanced diet.

Vitamin C is an example of a vitamin ▶ that is needed for a healthy diet. This vitamin is found in fresh fruit and vegetables. A few hundred years ago, when sea travel was very slow, sailors could not get fresh food. They often lacked vitamin C in their diet and came down with a disease called scurvy. Lack of vitamin C can also cause bleeding gums and changes in bones. Vitamin C can be lost from food if it is overcooked.

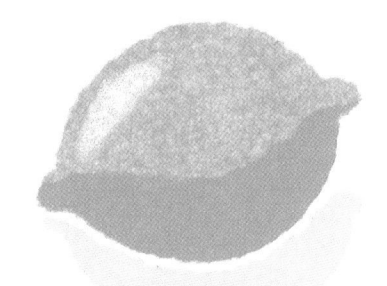

There are a large number of people in the world who do not eat meat. Many think that it is cruel to animals to keep them and then kill them. People who do not eat meat are called vegetarians. Protein in a vegetarian diet comes mainly from beans and nuts.

Around the world there ▶ are many different types of food, and some places are famous for a special type of dish. This is a common food in Spain called paella. It contains rice and seafood. In many parts of Asia, the dishes are often spicy, with curries being well-known examples.

◀ Keep a diary of the food you eat during a week. If possible, write down whether the food contains proteins, fats, carbohydrates, vitamins, or minerals. Information about this is often found on food containers. After a week, add up how much food you have eaten and decide whether you have a balanced diet. Make a list of the different countries that the foods may have come from.

STAYING HEALTHY

Some chemicals that people take into their bodies can be very harmful, as the body is not able to handle them.

Smoking gets smoke and ▶ tar into the lungs of the smoker—just compare the healthy lung on the left with the smoker's blackened lung on the right. Many smokers also develop lung diseases like bronchitis or lung cancer. Cigarette smoke can be very unpleasant for people who do not smoke. It is also a health risk because they breathe in some of the poisonous smoke. Many places, such as movie theaters and restaurants, have smoke-free areas.

Alcohol is a drug that can be harmful,  which is why it is against the law in many countries to sell alcohol to people under a certain age. After drinking, the alcohol easily passes through the stomach to the blood, and then it moves to the brain. Small amounts can make a person feel relaxed and happy. Larger amounts cause drunkenness and dizziness. It is very dangerous to drive after drinking, because alcohol makes people react more slowly than usual.

Drinking small amounts of alcohol may not damage your body. However, in large amounts it can kill brain cells and damage the liver, which is the part of the body that removes poisons.

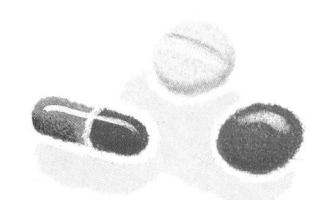

In some countries, such as Saudi Arabia, it is illegal for religious reasons to buy or drink alcohol. The punishments for those caught are very serious.

There are many types of drugs. If a ▲ drug has been made to help with an illness it is called a medicine, and it is safe to take in the prescribed amount. If a drug is not a medicine, it is probably dangerous. It is up to the individual person to make sure that his or her body is not damaged by taking in any harmful chemicals.

◀ Keep all medicines out of the reach of young children. Candies and tablets can be very hard to tell apart.

BREATHING

The oxygen that cells need to stay alive comes from the air. The air passes into your body through your nose and mouth. From there it moves to your lungs through the windpipe.

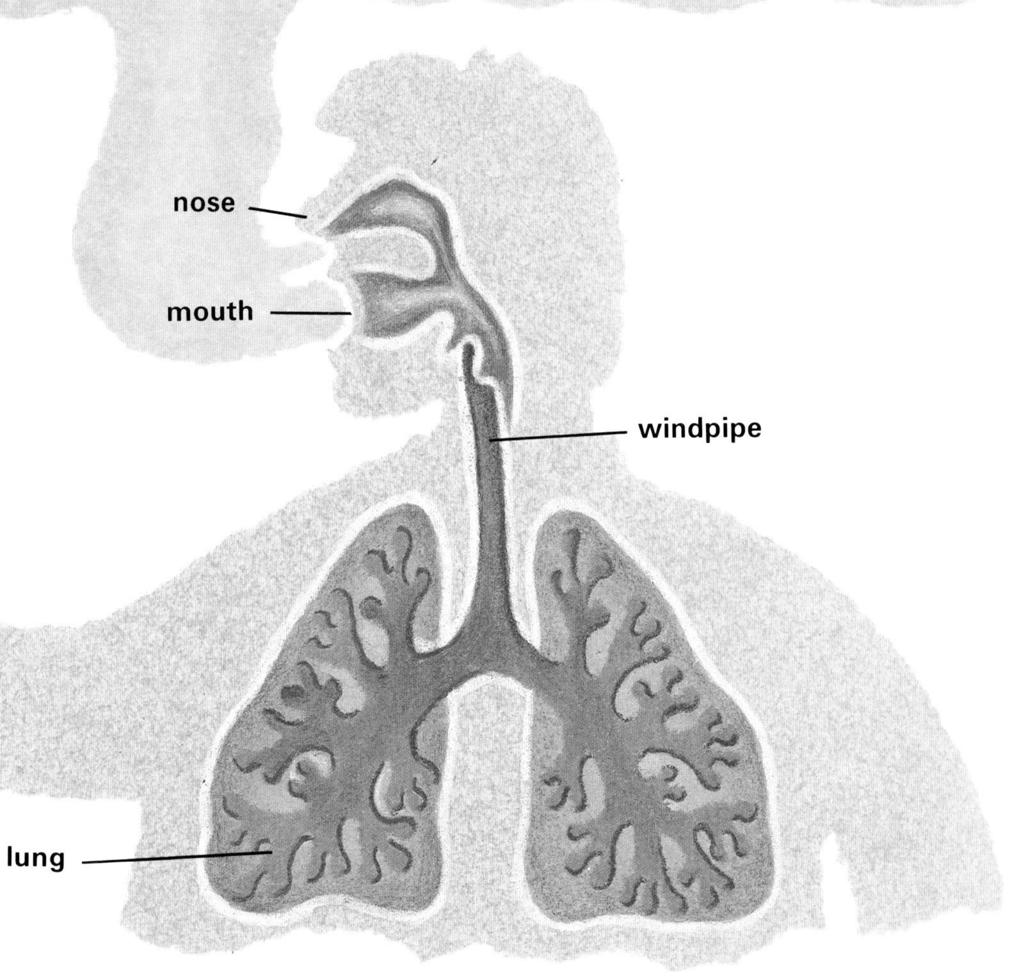

nose

mouth

windpipe

lung

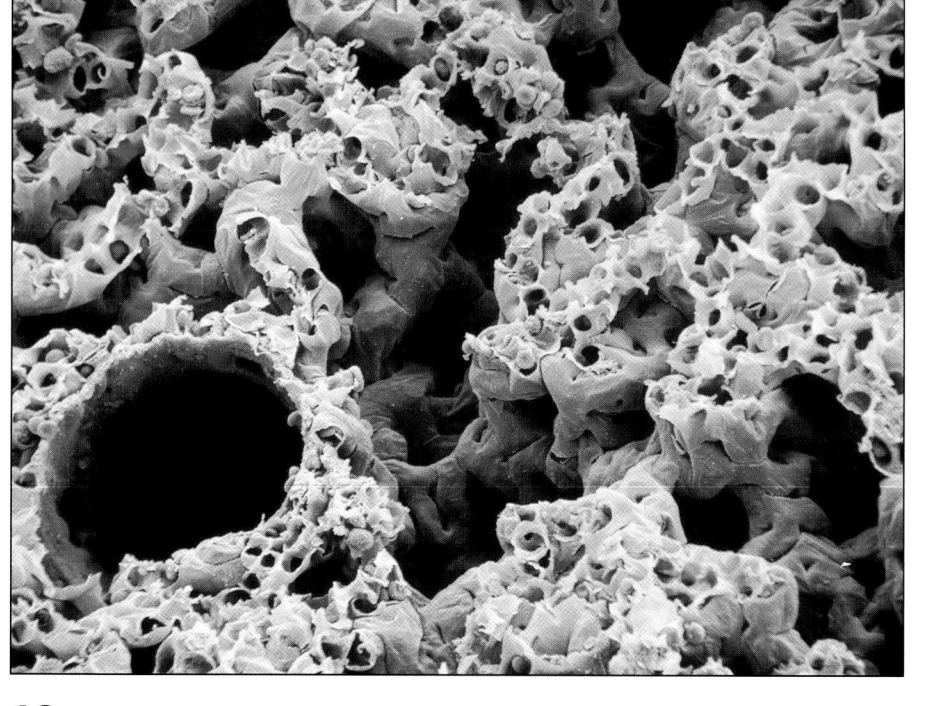

◄ The oxygen in the air passes through the lung walls into the blood. To help the oxygen do this, the lungs are spongy, with a large surface area, as you can see in this photograph (false color has been added). Cells also have to get rid of a waste gas called carbon dioxide. This passes from the blood back into the lungs, and you breathe it out.

It is very unhealthy to breathe air that is polluted. Dust and poisonous gases can damage the lungs. Cars and trucks give out harmful gases. Living in towns and cities that have a lot of traffic can give people illnesses. Some cities, such as Los Angeles, Tokyo, Athens, and Bangkok (pictured here), have serious air pollution problems.

Many people have jobs that can bring them into contact with very dirty air. Some mines and factories are full of dust and gases that are harmful to breathe. In fact, many miners have had to retire early because of lung problems. It is possible to wear masks that will filter out some of these chemicals.

Some people have a breathing problem called asthma. During an asthma attack, the tiny air tubes inside the lungs become narrower. Less oxygen can enter the blood, and this can make the person gasp for air. Some breathing problems can also be caused by bacteria and viruses which can infect the lungs. Influenza and tuberculosis are two examples. Before modern medicines, these and other diseases were big killers.

Other breathing problems occur in high places, such as on top of a mountain. High above sea level, the air is thinner and has less oxygen in it. Trying to move can quickly make a person short of breath. For this reason, mountain climbers have to be very careful. People who live at high altitude, like these Sherpas of Nepal, have thicker blood that carries more oxygen to help them cope with the thinner air found in the mountains.

THE BLOOD

The food and oxygen that are needed by all of your cells are taken around your body in blood. Each of the different parts of the blood does a different job. The important job of carrying the oxygen is done by millions of red cells. These are disk-shaped and give the blood its red color. Blood also has white cells. These are fewer in number than the red cells but are just as important. They help the body to fight diseases. This photograph has had false color added so that it is easy to tell the red from the white cells. Food, dissolved, is carried in the watery part of the blood, which is called plasma. ▼

To make sure that blood reaches all parts of your body, it is pumped by your heart. The blood passes to the rest of the body through tubes called arteries. Because the arteries have to stand up to the force of the pumping blood, they have thick walls. Each time the heart squeezes, we call it a heartbeat.

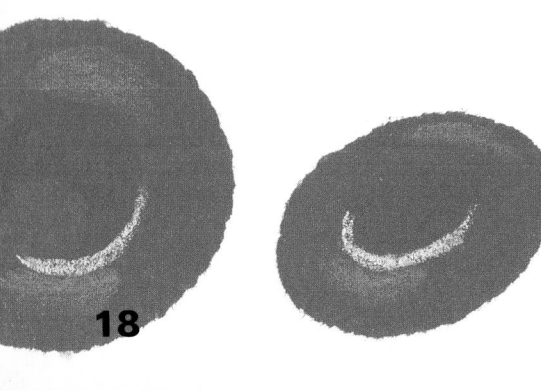

The blood reaches the farthest parts of the body by passing through thinner and thinner tubes. The thinnest of these are called capillaries. The blood returns to the heart along veins. The blood in the veins is not being forced by the heart any more, so veins do not need thick walls. They do need valves, however, to keep the blood from flowing the wrong way.

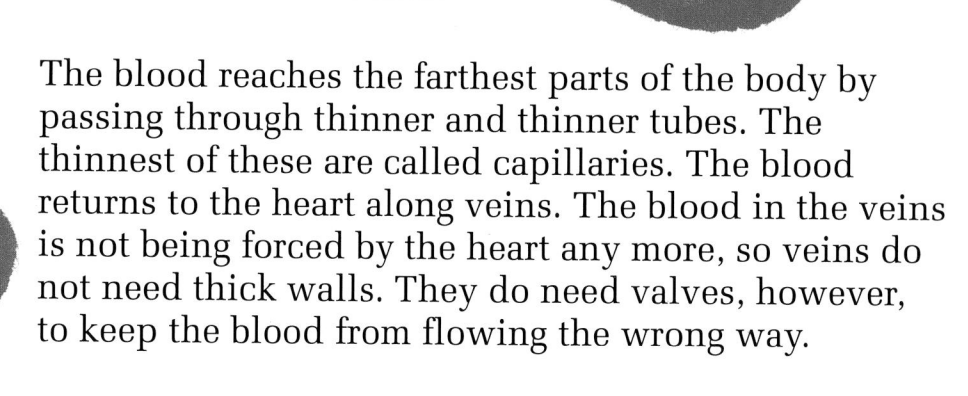

You can measure your heartbeat by taking your pulse where an artery is found near the skin. One of the easiest places is your wrist. The pump of the blood can be felt with a finger—don't use your thumb as it has its own pulse. The number of times your heart pumps per minute is called the pulse rate. Pulse rates vary. A normal pulse rate for a baby would be about 120 beats per minute. For an adult a normal rate would be about 70 beats per minute.

In the fifth century B.C., the Greeks thought that the veins carried blood and the arteries carried air. People believed this for nearly five hundred years, until Claudius Galen, a scientist who lived from A.D. 130—200, showed that the arteries were filled with blood. He found this out after working as a doctor treating gladiators, who frequently suffered from severe wounds. ▶

REMOVING WASTE

As your cells break down food, they produce substances that the body does not want. Some are actually poisonous, so your body has to get rid of them. A lot of the food you eat is not used by the body, so this must also be removed.

Solid waste material passes from the large intestine into the rectum. It leaves from the rectum when you go to the toilet. Mixed with the solid waste are a lot of bacteria. It is possible to catch diseases from the bacteria, so it is very important to wash your hands when you have been to the toilet.

Unwanted chemicals in the blood are filtered out through the kidneys. The kidneys are full of tiny tubes that allow water and small waste chemicals to pass through. The liquid waste, called urine, is stored in the bladder. When this gets full, the water passes out through the urethra.

The solid and liquid waste produced by humans should be treated before it is put into rivers and seas. This is done to remove the bacteria and viruses. The treatment is carried out at a sewage plant. Up until the middle of the last century, sewage was not treated in Britain. Many people died because they drank water that was contaminated with sewage.

◀Today, people sometimes become very ill from swimming in polluted water, because in some places untreated poisonous sewage is still piped out to sea.

▲ It is easy for drinking water to become contaminated. Floods, droughts, and wars can mean that many people have to live in a very small area. Treating sewage under these conditions can be almost impossible. Fresh water has to be brought in, and medical teams must try to protect the people against dangerous diseases, such as cholera.

Design a Poster

Imagine that you are living in a big city 150 years ago. Design and make a poster that would explain to people why they should not drink water that may have sewage in it.

THE SENSES

Humans usually have five senses. These are sight, hearing, taste, touch, and smell. Our eyes are the part of our body that let us see. A soft jellylike lens focuses light onto a light-sensitive layer of cells at the back of the eye. Nerves then send messages to the brain about what is being seen.

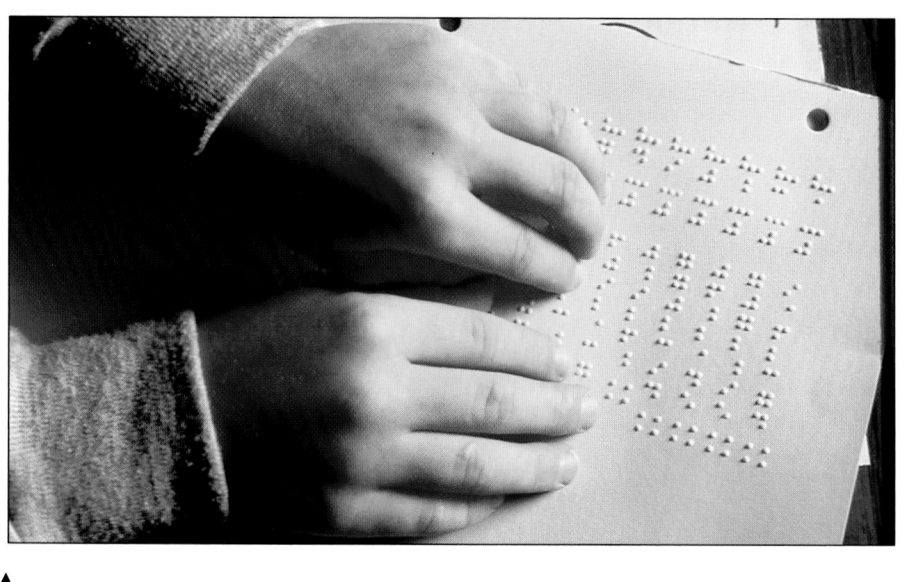

▲ There are many people who live and work normally despite not being able to see. Many inventions have helped them to read and to move about safely. Reading is done by feeling raised dots that make up a special code. This type of writing is called Braille after Louis Braille, who invented it.

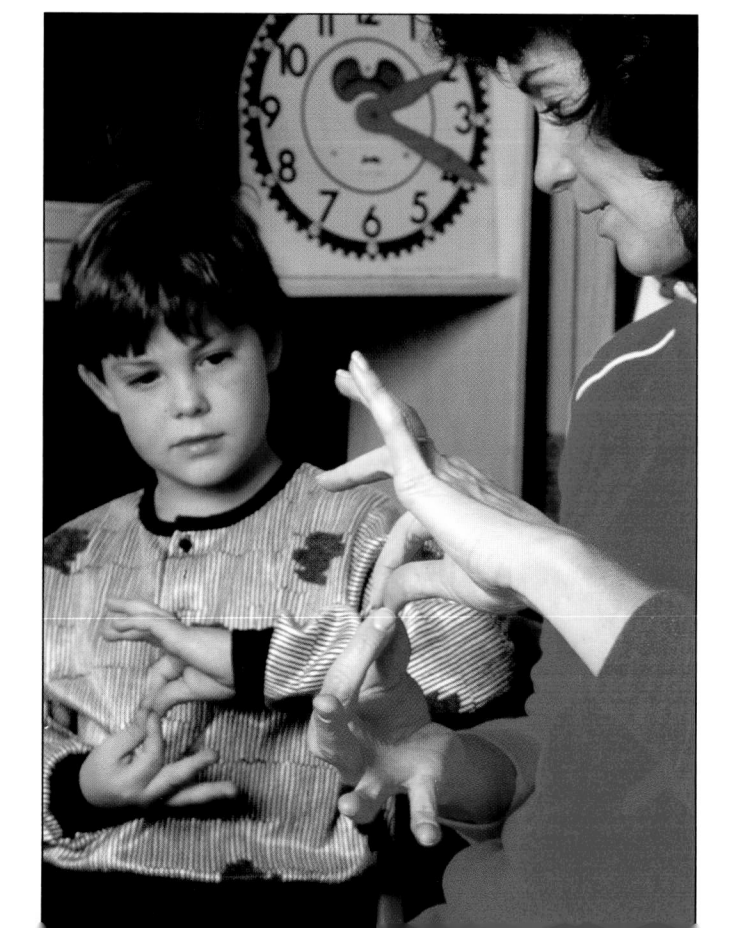

Sound is picked up by our ears. Inside each ear is a tight skin disk called the eardrum. This vibrates backward and forward like a drum when sound waves hit it. The movement is picked up by tiny bones that make the movement bigger. The bigger movement is then felt by tiny hairs in a curly, shell-like part of the ear. The movement of the hairs is sensed by nerves that send messages to the brain about the sound.

◄ People without hearing can lead normal lives. Small hearing aids can be put into their ears to make sounds louder. They may also be able to listen using sign language or reading the lips of a person who is speaking.

Touch sensors are found in our skin. Nerve endings detect things such as sharp objects and heat. Without these sensors, it would be possible to cut or burn parts of the body without feeling it. Taste is another important sense. By tasting food we can tell whether or not it is fresh. However, it is possible to fool our senses.

Fool Your Taste Buds ▶

1 Collect a few pieces of food, for example, chopped potato, onion, and apple.
2 Blindfold some friends, and do not let them smell the food.
3 Let them guess which flavors they are tasting. How easy was it for them to guess the flavors?

Smell is noticed by tiny hairs at the back of the nose. The smell of food helps our digestion by making our mouths water when we smell something delicious. Perfume can cover up unpleasant odors.

A)

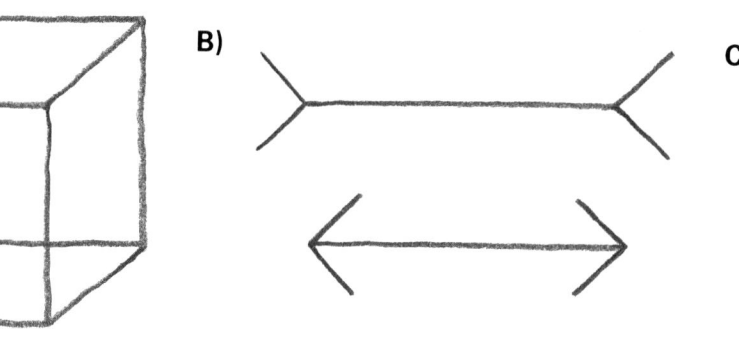

B)

C)

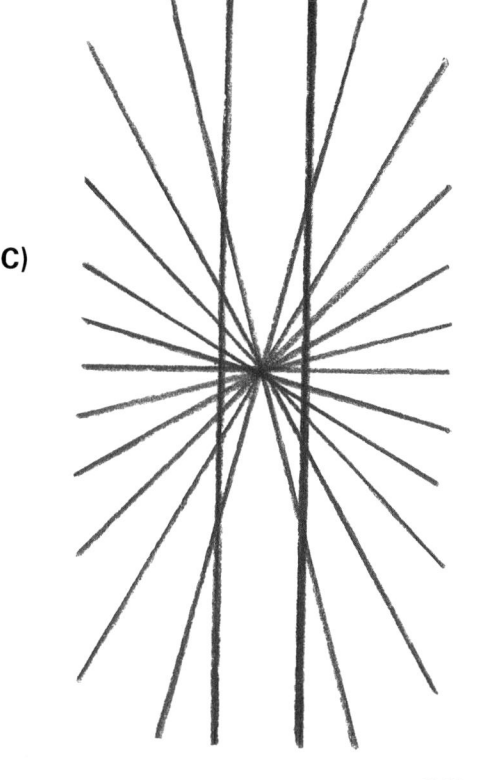

Fool Your Eyes ▲

A Is the dot at the front or back of the cube?
B Are the lines the same length?
C Are the heavy lines straight or curved?

(Answers on page 31)

THE BRAIN

Most of the messages from the body are sent to the brain. This is the organ that makes sense of the information coming from inside and outside your body. It is like a computer that controls everything the body does. The brain can either store information in the memory or can do something right away if it is needed. What should be done is decided on in a fraction of a second. Different parts of the brain control different parts of your body. ▶

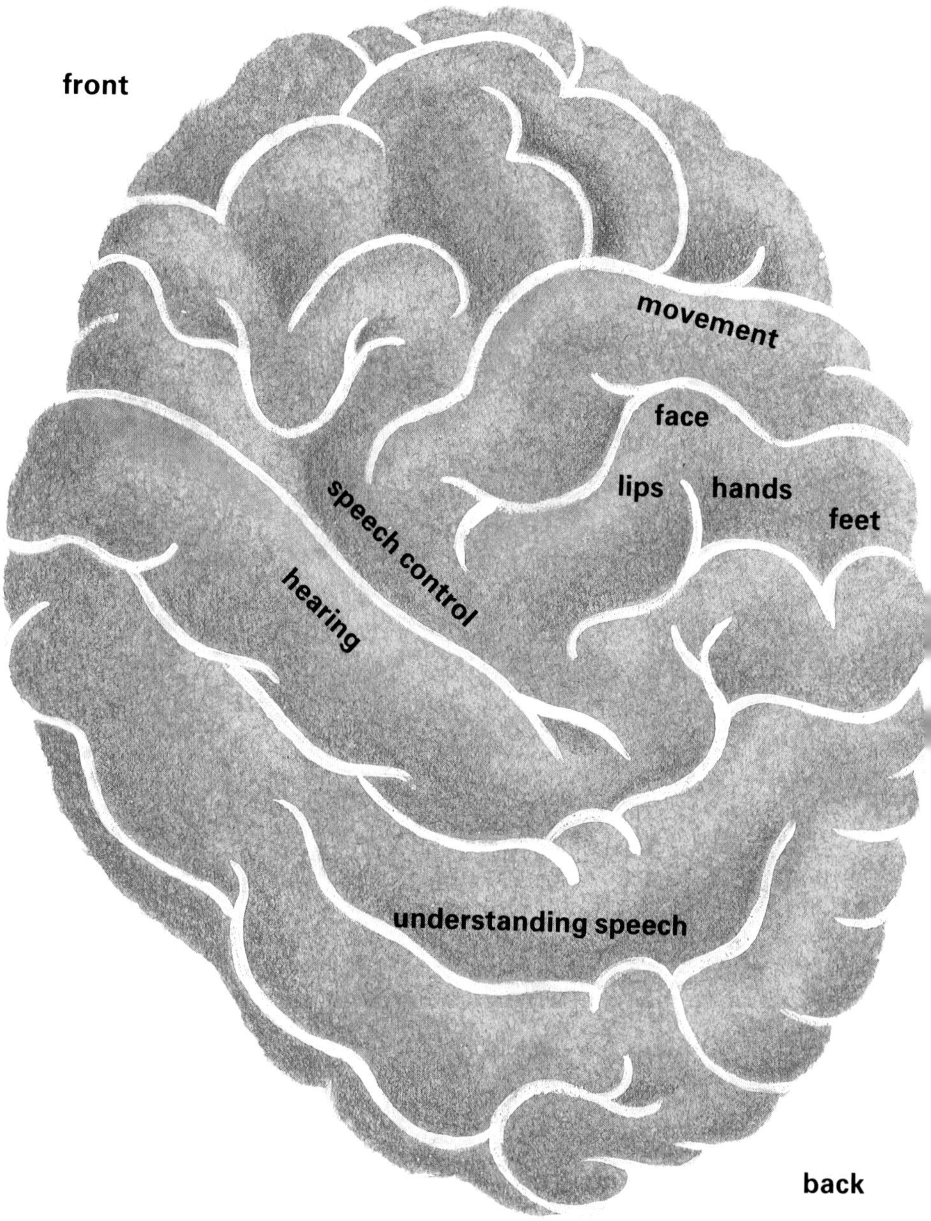

front

movement

face

lips   hands

feet

speech control

hearing

understanding speech

back

The messages to and from the brain travel along the nerves. The nerves form a network throughout the body that lets electrical messages pass along them. You can think of the nervous system as being like the telephone wires that link together all the rooms inside a big building. However, nerves are different because the message doesn't flow down them like a wire, but jumps from one nerve cell to another. The nerve cells are very thin but can be very long.

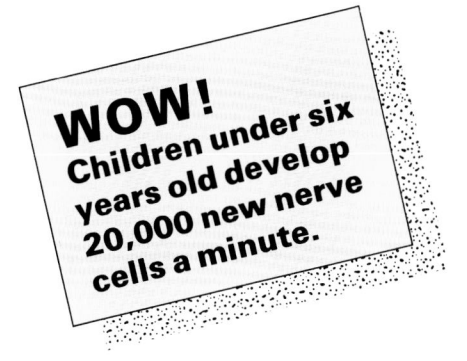

WOW! Children under six years old develop 20,000 new nerve cells a minute.

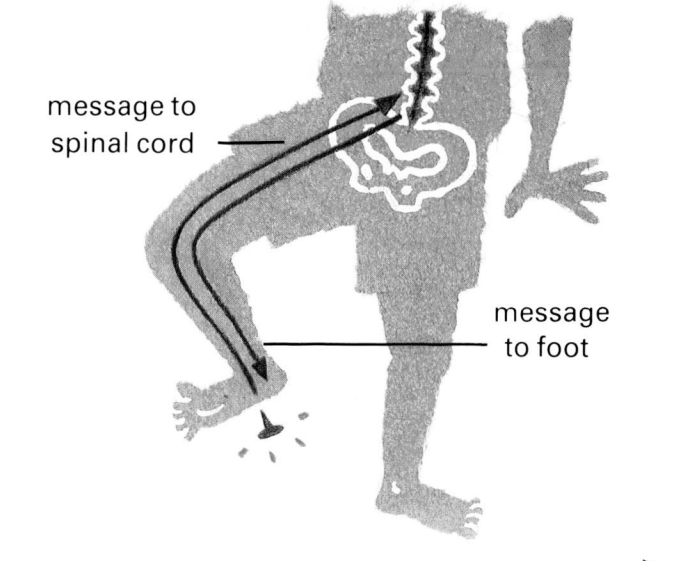

message to spinal cord

message to foot

Many parts of your body work without your being aware of them. You do not have to keep telling yourself to breathe or your heart to beat. All this is controlled by your brain.

◀ In emergencies, your body allows the brain to be skipped. For example, if you stand on a pin, the spinal cord inside your backbone sends a message to your muscles to lift your foot quickly.

Your brain has to work very hard when ▶ you run around playing games and sports. To throw and catch a ball needs hundreds of tiny muscle movements that have to be learned carefully and done over and over again. Imagine how many decisions the brain has to make for a person to ride a bike, compete in a pole vault event, or perform in a play. Everyday skills that we take for granted also need the complicated nervous system. How else would you be reading this book?

Test Your Memory ▶
1 With a group of friends, place some articles on a large tray.
2 Study the articles for one minute.
3 Ask one player to leave the room while you remove one article from the tray.
4 Let the person return and try to figure out which article is missing.
5 Each take a turn.

25

FIGHTING DISEASE

Many of the diseases ▶ that make us ill are caused by tiny organisms. They are called bacteria and viruses, and you can only see them by using a very powerful microscope. This is an influenza virus seen through a microscope.

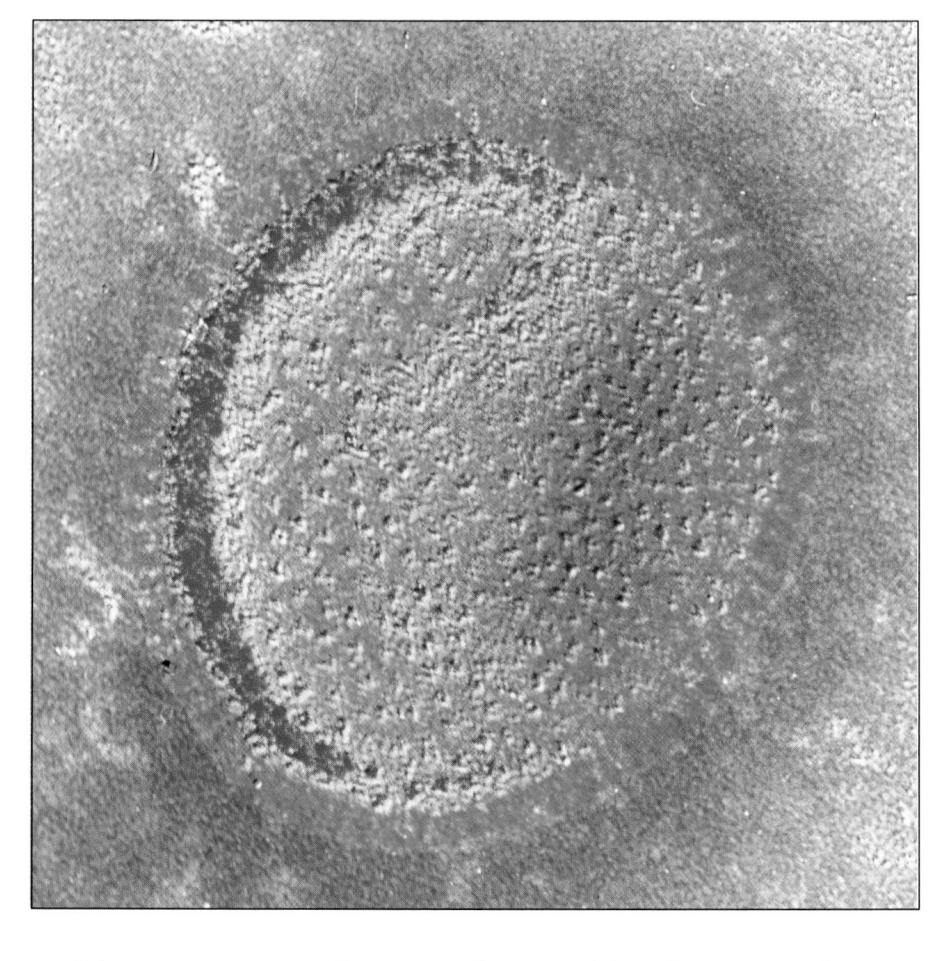

The theory that disease is caused by germs was first put forward in the 1860s by a French scientist named Louis Pasteur. Before this time, people did not really know what caused diseases. They regarded illness as the will of God and simply waited to see whether they would get better or die.

◀ Many discoveries that we think of as modern were actually made earlier in other parts of the world. The Hindu people in India have long known how to use infected fluids from the body of a sick person to inoculate other people against the disease. This technique was not used in Europe until 1796, when English physician Edward Jenner (pictured here) inoculated a small boy with cowpox as a protection against smallpox.

Many herbal remedies have been ▶ known for thousands of years. Poppy juice contains morphine and codeine and has been used as a painkiller for over 4,000 years. A plant called henbane provides us with a medicine called hyoscine. This is still used to help put people to sleep for operations, but it was known to the Babylonians as long ago as 2500 B.C.

A

antibody

nucleus

invader

white cell

The body is able to defend itself against many diseases. Bacteria and viruses can be destroyed by the white cells in the blood.

B

◀ Antibodies are another line of defense. These are chemicals that are produced when a bacteria or virus enters the body. The antibody sticks to the invader, which makes it harmless. The invader is then destroyed by a white cell. The antibodies remain in the body, making it less likely that the disease will be caught twice.

C

D

invader is destroyed

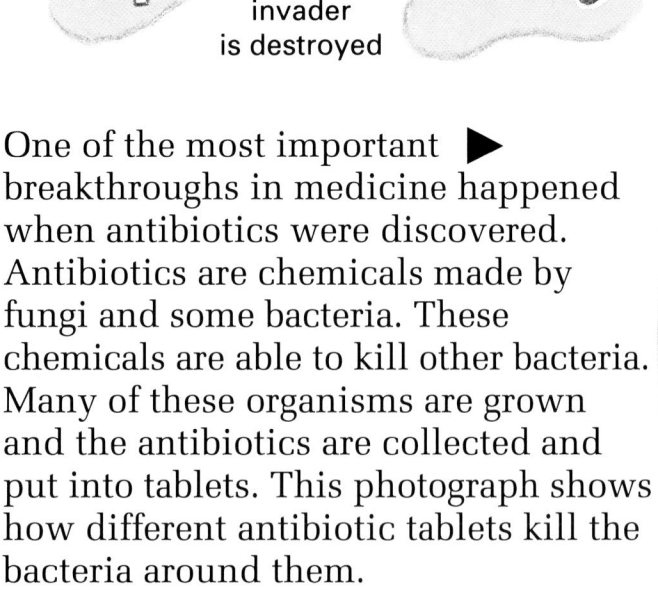

One of the most important ▶ breakthroughs in medicine happened when antibiotics were discovered. Antibiotics are chemicals made by fungi and some bacteria. These chemicals are able to kill other bacteria. Many of these organisms are grown and the antibiotics are collected and put into tablets. This photograph shows how different antibiotic tablets kill the bacteria around them.

Have you noticed that when you exercise you become out of breath? This is because your muscles are using up oxygen very quickly so that they can burn up food for energy. To get more oxygen into your lungs, you have to breathe more often and more deeply.

So that the extra oxygen in your lungs ▶ can get to your muscles more quickly, your heart starts to beat faster. This increase in the beating of your heart can be felt by taking your pulse—try it! When you exercise, your pulse rate rises. In fact, in some people it can rise from 70 beats per minute to nearly 200.

Regular exercise makes your muscles grow stronger. Your heart also becomes stronger so it can pump more blood. This is why people who are physically fit tend to have slow pulse rates. Another way to test your fitness is to see how long it takes for your heart to slow down to normal after exercise. This is known as the recovery rate.

When we are really frightened, we breathe faster and our hearts beat faster. This happens so that as much blood as possible can be pumped to our muscles, making us ready for anything that might happen. The chemical that causes these changes is adrenalin. This chemical can make people do extraordinary things, such as jump ◀ long distances or lift heavy weights.

Riskier sports have become popular in recent years. There are now more climbers and cavers than there have ever been, and many train to a very high level of fitness. It seems that the mix of exercise and excitement is just what they want.

Test Your Fitness
1 Take your pulse rate before you exercise. This is your resting pulse rate.
2 Exercise for two minutes.
3 Take your pulse for fifteen seconds every minute for ten minutes.
4 Every time you take your pulse multiply it by four to find out your pulse rate per minute.
5 Record your results on a graph.
6 How long does it take for your pulse rate to return to normal?▼

GLOSSARY

Adrenalin   A chemical made by the body to increase heart and breathing rates.

Antibiotics   Chemicals that kill bacteria. They are made by some fungi and are used as medicines.

Antibodies   Chemicals made in the body that fight infections.

Arteries   Thick-walled blood vessels in the body that carry blood, usually away from the heart.

Bone marrow   A substance found inside bones. It is where blood cells are made.

Capillaries   Very small blood vessels with thin walls.

Cartilage   A tough, smooth substance used to cover and cushion the ends of bones.

Cell   The smallest unit of life that can carry out all of the basic chemical reactions needed to live.

Digestion   The process by which food is broken down so that it can be taken into cells.

Enzymes   Chemicals made by the body to speed up chemical reactions, such as those used to break down food.

Intestines   The parts of the digestive system from the stomach to the anus.

Kidneys   The organs that filter out unwanted materials from the blood and control the level of water in the body.

Liver   The largest organ in the body. It does a large number of things including controlling the amount of glucose in the blood, breaking down old red blood cells, and storing iron.

Lungs   The organs we use for breathing. They are filled with many small tubes and air sacs to allow oxygen to pass into the blood and carbon dioxide to pass out of the blood.

Melanin   A dark pigment produced by the skin to protect the body from sunlight.

Membrane   The outer layer of the cells of the body. Membranes let some substances pass through them and block others.

Organ   A part of the body where cells and tissues are grouped together to do a particular job.

Tendons   Strips of tough material that join muscles to bones.

Tissues   Groups of cells of the same type that do the same job.

Urine   A mixture of water, urea, and salts that is produced by the kidneys and passed out as waste material from the body.

BOOKS TO READ

There are lots of topics in this book for you to explore further. Here are just a few suggestions for books to read to get you started:

Bershad, Carol and Bernick, Deborah. *Bodywork: The Kids' Guide to Food and Physical Fitness.* New York: Random House, 1981.

Collinson, Alan. *Choosing Health.* Facing the Future. Austin: Steck-Vaughn, 1991.

Condon, Judith. *Smoking.* Issues. New York: Gloucester, 1989.

Davies, Kay and Oldfield, Wendy. *Food.* Starting Science. Austin: Steck-Vaughn, 1992.

Nourse, Alan E., MD. *Lumps, Bumps, and Rashes: A Look at Kids' Diseases* (revised edition). First Books. New York: Franklin Watts, 1990.

Ward, Brian R. *Health and Hygiene.* Life Guides. New York: Franklin Watts, 1988.

Answers to optical illusions (page 23)
A It depends on which way your brain has interpreted the cube.
B The lines are the same length.
C The lines are straight.

INDEX